SPIES IN HISTORY

SPIES AND SPYING

KATE **WALKER** I ELAINE **ARGAET**

Smart Apple Media
1980 Lookout Drive
North Mankato
Minnesota 56003

Library of Congress Cataloging-in-Publication Data

Walker, Kate.
    Spies in history / by Kate Walker & Elaine Argaet.
    p. cm. — (Spies and spying)

    Includes index.
    Summary: Provides a brief overview of spies and espionage from the Bible to the early twentieth century, using examples from the Spanish Inquisition, the American Revolution, Tsarist Russia, and more.

    ISBN 1-58340-338-8
    1. Espionage—History—Juvenile literature. [1. Espionage—History. 2. Spies.] I. Argaet, Elaine. II. Title.
    III. Series.
    UB270.5.W3423 2003
    327.12—dc21   2002044621

First Edition
9 8 7 6 5 4 3 2 1

First published in 2003 by
MACMILLAN EDUCATION AUSTRALIA PTY LTD
627 Chapel Street, South Yarra, Australia, 3141

Associated companies and representatives throughout the world.

Copyright © Kate Walker and Elaine Argaet 2003

Edited by Miriana Dasovic
Text and cover design by Marta White
Maps and illustration on page 19 by Pat Kermode, Purple Rabbit Productions
Photo research by Jes Senbergs

Printed in Thailand

Acknowledgements

The author and the publisher are grateful to the following for permission to reproduce copyright material:

Cover photograph: Ivan the Terrible, courtesy of Art Archive; magnifying glass, courtesy of Getty Images; eye, courtesy of Ingram Royalty Free Image Library.

Archiv Gerstenberg, pp. 17, 27 (top); Art Archive, pp. 9, 11 (bottom), 17 (top); Australian Picture Library/Corbis, p. 27 (bottom); Bridgeman Art Library, pp. 9 (bottom), 15 (top); British Library, p. 7 (bottom); Cooee Historical Picture Library, pp. 13 (top), 19 (top); Getty Images, pp. 1, 3, 5 (bottom), 7 (top), 20, 21 (bottom), 25, 29 (top), 31, 32 (all); Ingram Royalty Free Image Library, pp. 1 (eye), 27 (top left); International Photographic Historical Organization, p. 29 (bottom); Mary Evans Picture Library, pp. 5 (top), 11 (top), 23 (bottom), 30 (center); Novosti (London), p. 4; © Prado Museum, Madrid, p. 13 (bottom); Radio Times Hulton Picture Library, p. 23 (top), in *Spies and Spymasters* by Jock Haswell, Thames and Hudson, London, 1977; Schalkwijk/Art Resource, p. 15 (bottom), New York, in *Conquistadors*, by Michael Wood, BBC Books, London, 2000; William L. Clements Library, University of Michigan, p. 28 (top).

While every care has been taken to trace and acknowledge copyright, the publisher tenders their apologies for any accidental infringement where copyright has proved untraceable. Where the attempt has been unsuccessful, the publisher welcomes information that would redress the situation.

CONTENTS

INTRODUCTION

A black tunic worn by one of Ivan the Terrible's dreaded Oprichniki spies in about 1560.

What is a spy?

A spy is a person who deals in secret information. Some spies gather the information, usually by sly means. Other spies carry the information from one person to another. There are spies who sit at desks and study the information, while other spies go out into the field and act on it. Some spies make up false information and spread it around to fool the enemy. Anyone who works secretly in this way is a spy.

- 👁 The proper name for spying is espionage.
- 👁 The modern name for a spy is an agent or intelligence officer.
- 👁 Information gathered by spies is called intelligence.

When did spying start?

People have been spying on each other since human history began. Army leaders have always known that the best way to defeat an enemy is to find out that enemy's weakness, and the best person to discover that weakness is a spy.

Why do people become spies?

Sometimes people become spies out of loyalty to their country. They gather information that will help keep their country safe. Sometimes people become spies because they know important secret information and sell it for money, usually a lot of money. Some people are tricked or forced into becoming spies. Other people choose to become spies because they find it exciting.

The first spies

In early times, spies crept up on the enemy and watched and listened. They gathered information and then crept quietly away. Some spies wrote down the information in code. Other spies found clever ways of hiding messages to keep them safe. Most spies worked for a rich spy master, who paid them and told them what to do.

Inventions change the art of spying

The art of spying changed in the 1800s when many marvellous new things were invented. Telegraph lines carried messages. The camera came into use. Spies started to use gadgets and learn special skills. They took photographs of the enemy and sent messages in Morse code. The world also became a richer place because of the invention of machines. A storekeeper with a talent for spying could become as wealthy and powerful as his spy master.

More changes in the world of spying

Spying changed again in the 1900s when bigger, more powerful weapons were made. Ships and trains that could transport thousands of people were built. Suddenly it was possible for the whole world to go to war. This meant that spying became a job for the government.

Russians find a Japanese spy trying to sneak into Port Arthur, China, in a coffin.

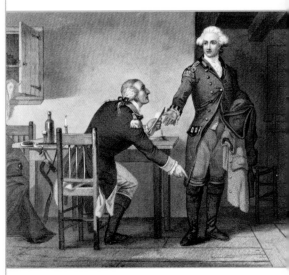

The traitor Benedict Arnold tells the spy John André to hide the secret papers in his shoe.

code	a secret language
gadgets	special tools
into the field	going into other countries to spy
Morse code	signals of dots and dashes that represent letters of the alphabet
spy master	a person in charge of many spies

SPIES IN THE BIBLE

BACKGROUND

- The Israelite people lived as slaves in Egypt for hundreds of years.

- Moses persuaded the Egyptian ruler to let the Israelite people go free.

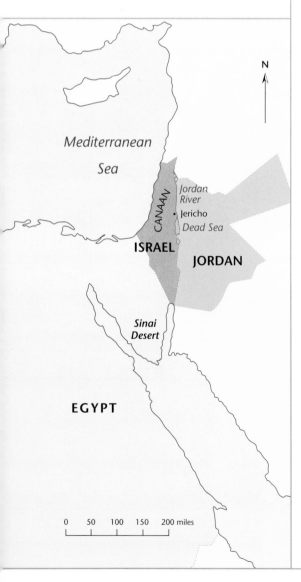

Moses: 12th century B.C.
Born: Egypt
Sent spies for the Israelites into Canaan

The Promised Land

Moses led the Israelites out of Egypt. They marched across the Sinai Desert towards a long, green valley called Canaan. For hundreds of years, Israelite prophets had said that Canaan was to be the Israelites' homeland. It was known as the Promised Land. However, other people already lived in Canaan, on farms and in towns. If the Israelites wanted this land, they would have to fight for it.

The 12 spies

Moses sent 12 spies into Canaan to get information about the land and its people. The spies came back and said that the land was so rich and green it "flowed with milk and honey." There was also bad news. The people living there, the Canaanites, were strong warriors and had built walls around their cities. Two of the spies, Caleb and Joshua, were tough soldiers. They told Moses that the Israelites could beat the Canaanites. The other 10 spies warned against it. They said that the Canaanites were giants, and would trample the Israelites like grasshoppers. This frightened the Israelite people, who howled death threats at Moses for bringing them into such danger. Moses led them away, and the Israelites wandered through the desert for the next 40 years.

Two of Moses's spies carry a bunch of grapes and pretend to be workmen while they spy on the land of Canaan.

The Israelites return to Canaan

Moses was an old man when the Israelites came back to Canaan to conquer it. Joshua was now in charge. He planned to attack the Canaanite city of Jericho, and sent two spies into the city. They were spotted, and darted into the house of a woman named Rahab. She knew who they were, and quickly took them to the roof and hid them under the flax she had spread out to dry. The king's guards came and searched Rahab's house, but they found no one.

The red rope

When the guards left, Rahab told the spies that her people were terrified of the Israelites. If the Israelites attacked the city, they would conquer it easily. Rahab offered to help the spies get away if they would help her in return. The spies agreed. Rahab lowered a red rope from her window and the spies climbed down the outside of the city wall. They told Rahab to hang this same red rope from the window when the battle began. The spies promised that the Israelite soldiers would see this rope and not harm anyone in the house. Joshua led the Israelites against Jericho and won the battle. Rahab and her family stayed safe.

Rahab promises to help the spies escape if they will help her.

flax   a plant that is dried and woven into rope and mats

prophets   people who tell the future

THE ANCIENT GENERAL'S CLEVER SPIES

BACKGROUND

- Rome and Carthage were two great cities and each ruled over a mighty empire.

- At first, they agreed to share the world peacefully between them.

- In 264 B.C., they changed their minds and went to war.

Scipio Africanus: 237–183 B.C.
Born: Rome, Italy
Sent spies for Rome against Carthage

The young general

Scipio was just 25 years old when he became a general in the Roman army. At that time, a large Carthaginian force was marching through Spain and making for Rome, planning to attack the city from the north. Scipio took command of an army of just 11,000 Roman soldiers. He cleverly used this small force to drive the large Carthaginian army all the way back through Spain.

Scipio wanted to defeat the Carthaginians completely so they could never threaten Rome again. To do this, he would have to take his army across the sea to North Africa. Scipio worked on his battle plan for almost a year. He was determined to conquer the city of Carthage once and for all.

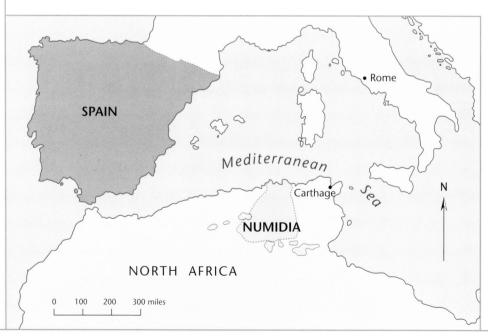

Roman troops in North Africa

Scipio landed his troops in North Africa and immediately sent a message to King Syphax of Numidia. King Syphax was friendly with the king of Carthage, and they had always helped each other in battle. Scipio's message said that he wanted to make a peace deal with the Numidians. In reality, Scipio wanted to get spies inside the Numidian camp to find out its weaknesses.

Meeting with the Numidians

King Syphax agreed to the meeting, and Scipio sent a group of Roman soldiers. Half of them were disguised as ordinary slaves. When the Romans arrived at the Numidian camp, one of King Syphax's men recognized one of the "slaves." He said that the man was not a slave at all but a Roman officer. The Roman group leader turned to the "slave" and slapped him across the face. He abused the man for even daring to look like a Roman soldier. The "slave" fell to the ground whimpering. No Roman soldier would ever act that way. This convinced the Numidians that the man was indeed just a slave.

Spying on the Numidians

During the peace talks, King Syphax kept all the Romans in one place. This did not suit the Romans, so they came up with a plan to get a better look at the camp. They did this by spooking one of their horses. The frightened animal took off, with all the Roman "slaves" running after it. The "slaves" kept the horse galloping through the camp until they had seen everything they wanted to see.

The peace talks ended and the Romans left the camp. Scipio's army attacked the Numidians soon afterwards. The Roman army was small but it defeated the Numidians easily. Scipio's spies had found out all the weak spots in the Numidian defenses. Scipio marched on Carthage next. He defeated the city.

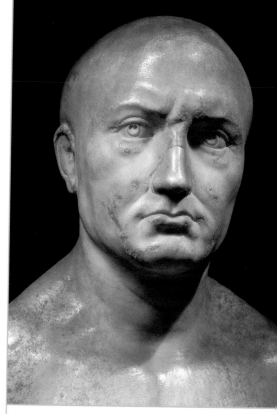

A statue of the head of Scipio Africanus.

Scipio's troops in battle.

empire   a large number of countries ruled by one powerful country

peace deal   an agreement not to fight

spooking   frightening

ENGLAND'S MEDIEVAL SPY KING

BACKGROUND

- The Vikings came from Norway and invaded England twice.

- The first time, they conquered much of northern England.

- The second time, they tried to conquer the south.

SCOTLAND

N

Danes defeated by Alfred A.D. 878

Alfred's base camp A.D. 878

London

Chippenham
Edington
Athelney   WESSEX

0   50   100   150 miles

Alfred the Great: A.D. 849–99
Born: Wessex, England
Spied for Wessex against the Vikings

The Vikings' surprise attack

In A.D. 878, King Alfred of Wessex was celebrating Christmas in his royal fortress at Chippenham. The Vikings attacked without warning. Many Wessex people were killed. Many others gave in to the Vikings because they were too afraid to do anything else. Young Alfred was lucky to escape with his life. He fled to an island base camp in the marshes of Athelney. A small band of 50 loyal knights went with him. Things looked bad for Alfred. He had very few soldiers, but he did have a plan.

The Vikings' winter camp

The Vikings did not bother to chase Alfred into the marshes. They thought he was already beaten. The leader of the Vikings, Guthrun, took over the fortress at Chippenham. Guthrun made it his winter camp and the Vikings spent two months there, eating, drinking, and enjoying themselves. When spring came, Guthrun called his commanders together and they started making battle plans for the year to come. The Vikings had grown soft over the winter. They were not in a hurry to take up their swords and start fighting again.

The minstrel in the Viking camp

A minstrel had wandered into the Viking camp during winter. He was a gifted young musician, and he sang tender love songs that the Vikings enjoyed. The Vikings threw this minstrel scraps of food in payment for his songs. When the Vikings were ready to take up their weapons once more, the young minstrel slung his harp over his shoulder and left.

King Alfred the Great.

King Alfred returns

The Vikings set out to march across Wessex and seize the rest of Alfred's kingdom. Alfred came out of the Athelney marshes and took the Vikings by surprise. Many of Alfred's loyal knights and soldiers were with him. A great battle was fought. The Vikings were beaten back into a ditch, where it was impossible for them to fight. The Vikings broke ranks and fled to Edington. They took shelter in an ancient fort there. Alfred's army surrounded them. The Viking leader was forced to surrender after only two weeks. The fort had no water and the Vikings were dying of thirst.

A minstrel with a harp, like the one used by Alfred.

King Alfred the Great

Guthrun was brought before Alfred. Young Alfred sat on his throne, strumming his harp. Guthrun immediately knew who the young man was. He was the minstrel who had sung love songs in the Viking camp while the Vikings had made their battle plans! This young king became known as Alfred the Great.

broke ranks	broke away from a well-ordered group
invaded	used force to enter someone else's land
marshes	wet and soggy land
minstrel	an old-fashioned singer or musician

SPIES OF THE INQUISITION

BACKGROUND

The Inquisition was an organization set up by the Catholic Church to hold trials and punish people for not obeying church rules.

Inquisition trials were held in different places in the world from 1250 to the early 1800s.

Saint Joan: 1412–31

Joan of Arc was 16 years old when she said that saints came to her and told her she was meant to lead the French army against the English. The French king gave Joan a suit of bright armor. She rode at the head of the French forces and led them to victory after victory. Then, in 1430, Joan was caught by the enemy.

Joan is spied on in prison

The English handed Joan over to a court of the Inquisition. She was put into prison and spies were put into the cells around her. One of these spies was a French priest who reported everything Joan said, even her prayers. The judge in charge of Joan's trial was a French bishop. He was also an English spy. The bishop asked Joan to sign a statement saying that she would never wear men's clothes or ride into battle again. Later, when the bishop read out the statement in court, it said something different. The statement said that Joan admitted to committing crimes against God. With this false document, the judge found Joan guilty of witchcraft. She was burned at the stake in the Old Market of Rouen on May 30, 1431.

The Spanish Inquisition

Juan Robles was a young Jewish glassmaker who lived in Spain. He had to pretend to be a Christian because the Inquisition sometimes put Jews to death for not believing in the Christian god of the Catholic Church. When Robles was 21 years old, he decided to leave Spain and go to Morocco. There he could follow his Jewish faith openly.

His mother missed him and wrote to him, begging him to come home. She was also a Jew who pretended to be a Christian. Robles wrote back and told his mother his plan. He was going to move from place to place in Morocco, change his name, and slowly make his way back to Spain.

Robles paid a group of traveling merchants to carry his letters to his mother. The merchants were really part of the Inquisition's large network of spies, so they gave the letters to the Inquisition first. A Christian monk in Morocco made friends with Robles and advised him to go home. He said that if Robles would give himself up to the Inquisition, the monk would speak on Robles's behalf at the trial. The monk was also a spy.

Robles is tried by the Inquisition

The Inquisition got tired of waiting for Robles and held a trial without him. The judges used Robles's letters as evidence against him, and found him guilty of believing in a false god. They made an effigy of Robles and burned it in place of burning him.

Robles kept his promise to his mother. Years later, he returned safely to Spain using another name.

Joan of Arc in armor.

An Inquisition trial.

armor	metal clothing that protects the body
effigy	a model of a person
evidence	facts that prove the truth

LA MALINCHE, THE AZTEC SPY

BACKGROUND

- The Spanish conquistadors invaded Mexico in 1519.

- Mexico at that time was ruled by a powerful Indian tribe called the Aztecs.

La Malinche: 1495–1540
Born: Veracruz, Mexico
Spied for the Spanish conquistadors against the Mexican Indians

The daughter of an Aztec chief

La Malinche was a small child when her father died. Her mother married again, and La Malinche's stepfather gave her to a wandering tribe of Veracruz Indians. He was afraid that La Malinche might become more important than his own children because her father had been a chief. A few years later, the Veracruz Indians sold La Malinche to the Tabasco Indians. La Malinche grew up learning to speak several different Indian languages.

The Spanish conquistadors arrive

La Malinche was a young woman when the conquistadors landed in Mexico. Their leader was Hernán Cortés. The Tabasco Indians were one of the first tribes to surrender to him. As a peace offering, the Tabasco Indians gave the Spaniards 20 women to do their washing and cooking. La Malinche was one of these women.

She quickly learned to speak Spanish, so Cortés made her his translator. La Malinche traveled with Cortés. She spoke to the Indians for him, and told him what the Indians said in reply. La Malinche soon fell in love with Cortés and became his spy. She told him when the Indians were lying and what the Indians said when they talked among themselves.

Gulf of Mexico

N

MEXICO

Tenochtitlan

Veracruz

Pacific Ocean

0 100 200 300 400 miles

Aztec empire

Cortés and the Aztecs

Cortés had arrived in Mexico with only 508 soldiers. The Indians could have easily beaten him. La Malinche helped Cortés by convincing many Indian tribes to join forces with him. She told the Indians that the Spaniards would help them defeat their old enemy, the Aztecs. The Aztecs were a fierce tribe who sacrificed Indians from other tribes to their Aztec gods.

In August 1519, the Spaniards began a long and difficult march towards the Aztec capital, Tenochtitlan (now called Mexico City). Each day, more Indians from different tribes joined them. Cortés finally reached Tenochtitlan with thousands of Indian warriors behind him, ready to fight with the Spanish.

Cortés came face-to-face with the Aztec chief, Montezuma. Luckily, La Malinche was there to translate what Montezuma said. "Welcome," he declared, "we have been waiting for you. This is your home." The Aztecs believed that one of their lost gods would come back from over the sea one day. Montezuma thought that Cortés was this god. The Aztecs welcomed the Spanish into their city.

La Malinche translates between Cortés and Montezuma.

The great Aztec city of Tenochtitlan.

La Malinche's reward

Cortés gave La Malinche three towns as payment for helping him conquer Mexico and its many Indian tribes. La Malinche wanted to marry Cortés, but he already had a wife back in Spain.

conquistadors Spanish soldiers who conquered Central America in the 1500s

convincing making a person believe that what you say is true

translator a person who changes one language into another

RUSSIA'S THOUSAND SPIES

BACKGROUND

- In the late 1500s, Tsar Ivan IV drove the feared Mongol hordes out of Russia.

- He then filled the Russian countryside with his own terrible spies.

- Every Russian Tsar after Ivan IV had a large army of spies.

Ivan the Terrible: 1530–84

Ivan was a prince who was crowned Tsar of Russia at the age of 16. He ruled well for 13 years. Then Ivan went insane. He became a cruel ruler, and was soon known as Ivan the Terrible. Ivan set up a special police force to act as his bodyguards. They were called the Oprichniki, and they rode black horses and dressed in black robes. The Oprichniki had a picture of a dog's head and a broom on their saddles. The dog's head showed that they bit like dogs, and the broom showed they would sweep the land clean.

Russia during the reign of Nicholas II

The Oprichniki at work

Ivan did many evil deeds. Once, he sent his Oprichniki into the town of Novgorod to spy on everyone. The Oprichniki quickly found 3,000 people who they claimed were plotting against Ivan's life. These 3,000 people were put to death. With so many bodies lying about, a plague broke out. This plague killed another 60,000 people. The whole town of Novgorod was destroyed in less than a month. Ivan soon became frightened of the Oprichniki himself and disbanded them.

Ivan the Terrible.

More spies of the Russian Tsars

In 1796, Tsar Paul became ruler of Russia. He gave everyone in the land a chance to be a spy. A yellow box was placed outside the palace gates. Anyone could slip a note into this box, to reveal secrets about someone else. Tsar Paul got many notes this way, but not much good information. One note resulted in the arrest of an officer for wearing his hat at the wrong angle!

In 1826, Tsar Nicholas I set up a secret police force to protect himself and his family. This spy force was called the Okhrana. It was the biggest spy network in history up to that time. The Okhrana had enough members to put a spy in every Russian home.

The spy Ievno Azeff enjoying himself with a friend.

Spies of the last Russian Tsar

Nicholas II was the last Tsar of Russia and he had 100,000 spies. They spied mostly on students who were unhappy with his leadership and wanted him off the throne. One of these spies was Ievno Azeff. He spied on students by becoming a trusted member of their secret groups. Azeff found out their names and urged them to do dangerous things, such as building bombs. With this information, the secret police could catch the students in the act and arrest them all. Azeff went from group to group, making friends and then betraying them.

disbanded   when a group is broken up

Mongol   people from Mongolia

plague   a deadly disease that spreads from person to person

Tsar   a Russian king

WALSINGHAM, SPY MASTER FOR QUEEN ELIZABETH I

Sir Francis Walsingham: 1532–90
Born: Norfolk, England
Spied for Queen Elizabeth I, a Protestant, against Mary, Queen of Scots and King Philip II of Spain, both Catholic

BACKGROUND

- Elizabeth I was queen of England from 1558 to 1603.

- Many Catholic people in England did not want a Protestant queen, and they plotted against her.

A dangerous rival

In 1568, the Protestant lords of Scotland removed Mary, Queen of Scots from the throne. She fled to England in fear of her life. There she asked Queen Elizabeth, her second cousin, to protect her. Mary was second in line to the English throne. Elizabeth knew that Mary would try to kill her and take the English throne for herself.

The beer barrel plot

Elizabeth locked Mary in a country house and kept her prisoner there. Mary still found a way of getting messages to and from her Catholic friends. These friends were willing to help Mary get rid of Protestant Queen Elizabeth. Each day, Mary received a barrel of beer. Secret notes were hidden inside the bung holes of the barrels. In these notes, Mary and her friends hatched a plot to kill Elizabeth.

Mary did not know that the man who brought the beer was really a spy. He worked for Sir Francis Walsingham, Queen Elizabeth's chief adviser and spy master. Clever Walsingham let Mary go on sending and receiving messages until he had proof, in her own handwriting, of what she and her friends were planning to do. For plotting to kill the queen, Mary was beheaded in 1587.

N

SCOTLAND

ENGLAND

Norfolk

FRANCE

ITALY

SPAIN

Cádiz

Mediterranean

Sea

0 100 200 300 400 500 miles

The Spanish threaten to invade England

The Catholic king of Spain, Philip II, vowed to pay back the English for Mary's death. He began building a large fleet of ships, which he called his Armada. Philip planned to use the Armada to invade England.

Walsingham's spies in Spain

Spy master Walsingham sent spies into Spanish seaports to find out how big this Armada was, and what port it would sail from. Walsingham gave this information to Sir Francis Drake, the commander of the English navy. Drake made a daring raid on Cádiz Harbor, where he set fire to most of the Spanish ships. Philip of Spain asked Italian bankers for loans of money to rebuild his fleet. Walsingham sent spies to find out which bankers Philip had asked. Walsingham then bribed these bankers to make the payments slowly. This gave England more time to prepare its own fleet of ships.

Walsingham's Armada spy

Walsingham's best spy was a young Englishman named Anthony Standen. Standen knew he would be caught if he went to Spain to spy on the Armada. Instead, he went to Italy and made friends with the Italian ambassador. The Italian ambassador then visited Spain and got his Italian staff to spy around the Spanish ports. These Italian spies sent Standen valuable information about the size of the Armada fleet and where it would sail from. With the help of this information, the much smaller English fleet easily defeated the mighty Armada.

Sir Francis Walsingham, spy master.

Bung holes

Wooden beer barrels used to have a hole in the side where the bung was hammered in.

ambassador   a person who officially represents a country

second in line   the next person to inherit the throne

SPIES OF THE AMERICAN WAR OF INDEPENDENCE

BACKGROUND

- The American War of Independence (1775–83) was fought between American settlers and British soldiers.

- The Americans did not want to be ruled by Britain any more. They wanted to become a nation and govern themselves.

Nathan Hale: 1755–76
Born: Connecticut, United States
Spied for the American settlers against the British

The teacher who became a spy

Nathan Hale was 19 years old when he left his job as a school teacher and joined the Connecticut militia. General George Washington asked if any of the militiamen would go to Long Island and spy on the British. Hale volunteered. On September 1, 1776, he dressed as a Dutch schoolmaster and slipped behind enemy lines. Hale was brave enough to go right into the British army camps. He took note of how many guns and soldiers the British had.

Hale was making his way back to the American camp when he was stopped and searched by British troops. When they found the secret information on him, Hale confessed that he was a spy. Next morning, September 22, he was hanged without a trial. Hale's dying words were, "I regret that I have but one life to give for my country."

Nathan Hale was the first American to be caught and executed for spying.

Benedict Arnold: 1741–1801
Born: Connecticut, U.S.
Tried to betray the Americans to the British

John André: 1750–80
Born: London, England
Spied for the British against the Americans

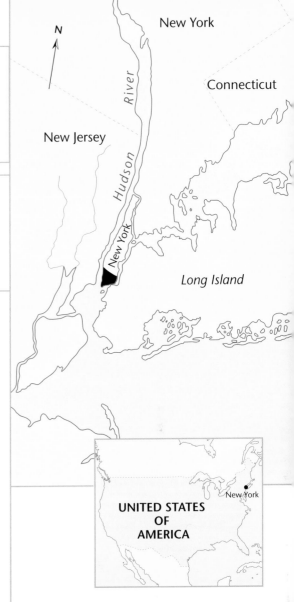

Benedict Arnold becomes a traitor

Benedict Arnold was a clever officer in the American army. He became angry when other officers got promoted to higher jobs over him. Arnold was in charge of the forts at West Point. These forts guarded the entrance to New York's Hudson River. Arnold sent a secret message to the British, offering to hand over these forts for £20,000. This was an enormous sum of money at the time.

The British agreed and sent a young English spy, Major John André, to meet him. André was a handsome adventurer who enjoyed the excitement of spying. Arnold gave André a set of plans that would help the British easily take the forts.

On September 23, 1780, André disguised himself as a merchant and set out to carry the plans back to his commander in the British camp. He was stopped by an American patrol. The soldiers searched him and found the plans hidden in his shoe. André offered to pay the soldiers £2 if they let him go. They refused. André was arrested, tried and executed.

Arnold heard that André had been caught, so he quickly left the Americans and joined the British army. When the Americans won the war, Arnold fled to England. He lived there for the rest of his life.

John André tries to bribe the American patrol.

militia   an army of people who are not professional soldiers

KARL SCHULMEISTER, SPY FOR EMPEROR NAPOLEON

BACKGROUND

- In 1793, the French people replaced their king with a government chosen by the people.

- During this time, a French general named Napoleon Bonaparte was winning great battles for France.

- Napoleon gained so much power that he crowned himself emperor of France in 1804.

Karl Schulmeister: 1770–1853
Born: Alsace, France
Spied for Napoleon against the French Royalists and Austria

From storekeeper to spy

Karl Schulmeister opened a small store in his hometown when he was just 17 years old. This store sold fancy food and other goods that were hard to get. Schulmeister bought many of these goods from thieves. He did not care about right or wrong. He just wanted to be rich.

Schulmeister soon saw that he could make more money from spying, so he offered to spy for the army. One of the jobs the army asked him to do was write a forged letter to the Duke d'Enghien, a French prince living safely in Germany. The army wanted to get rid of all these French princes in case one of them planned to return to France and make himself king.

The Duke d'Enghien had no such plans. When he got Schulmeister's letter, he believed it was from a young woman he knew. The letter asked him to meet with her. The duke came to the meeting and was seized by soldiers. They brought him back to France and executed him.

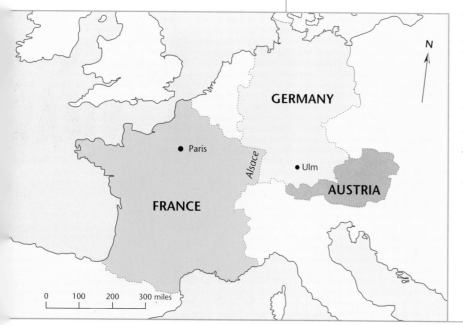

Schulmeister becomes the emperor's spy

Napoleon was eager to meet Schulmeister because he wanted someone clever to go to Austria and spy on the Austrian army for him. Schulmeister got the job and set to work forging papers again. He sent papers to the chief of the Austrian army. They said that Schulmeister was a Hungarian nobleman and that Napoleon was about to banish him from France. Schulmeister hinted that he had important information about the French army and would happily give it to the Austrians.

The Austrians believed him, and Schulmeister was soon working for them as chief of army intelligence. He sent back to Napoleon every piece of secret information he gathered. With the help of this information, Napoleon crushed the Austrian army in the Battle of Ulm in 1805.

Schulmeister's fate

Schulmeister was paid well for his work in Austria. He built a grand house for himself in Alsace and boasted openly of what he had done. However, by 1813 Napoleon and his army were being forced back to Paris by Austrian troops. The Austrians did not forget that Schulmeister had betrayed them all those years before. They sent soldiers with heavy cannons to destroy his house. To save his life, Schulmeister had to give the Austrian soldiers all the money he had. Years later, he went back to Alsace. There he lived in poverty for the rest of his life.

Karl Schulmeister.

The Austrians stand defeated before Emperor Napoleon after the Battle of Ulm.

banish	send away, never to return
forged	faked
poverty	poor living conditions

THE SPY WHO BETRAYED AN IRISH HERO

BACKGROUND

- From 1649, the people of Ireland lived under harsh English rule.

- In 1791, a group called the United Irishmen took up arms and tried to drive the English out.

Robert Emmet: 1778–1803
Born: Dublin, Ireland
Fought for Ireland against the English

The fight to free Ireland

Robert Emmet was an Irish patriot who joined the United Irishmen in 1798. He fought with them as they battled English soldiers in the streets of Dublin. The uprising failed, so Emmet and the other leaders had to flee to France. There they began planning a second uprising. They met with the French leader, Napoleon, who hinted that French troops might soon invade England. The Irishmen promised to help the French if the French would help them in return.

The traitor strikes

Emmet returned to Ireland in 1803 to get the people of Dublin ready for the second uprising. This time they would have French soldiers fighting on their side. Emmet began to store weapons in different houses around Dublin. When one of these houses was destroyed by a bomb, Emmet knew that his plans had been discovered. However, he had no idea who had betrayed him.

The second uprising was planned for July 23. The day came, but no French soldiers appeared. The other Irish groups who had promised to join in did not show up. Emmet's group marched on Dublin Castle alone. The English were waiting for them.

Betrayed by one of his own people

Emmet escaped to a hide-out near the home of his fiancée, Sarah Curran. He was now an outlaw and had to get out of Ireland. Sarah Curran promised to go with him to another land. They planned to sail to America and be married there. On August 25, English soldiers stormed the hide-out and arrested Emmet. He had been betrayed again.

His life in a traitor's hands

Sarah Curran's father was a lawyer, John Curran. He was a trusted friend of the Irish rebels, but he could not help Emmet for fear of putting his daughter's life at risk. Her unsigned love letters had been found hidden in Emmet's coat. John Curran got his law partner, Leonard MacNally, to defend Robert Emmet in court. MacNally was also a trusted friend of the rebels. No one blamed MacNally when Emmet was found guilty on September 19 and executed in public the following day.

Death of a traitor

When Leonard MacNally died years later, it was found that he had been receiving regular payments of £300 a year. All these payments were recorded in the British Secret Service Money Book. One large amount of £1,000 had been paid to MacNally on August 23, 1803, the day of Robert Emmet's capture.

A portrait of Robert Emmet, the Irish hero.

fiancée   a woman engaged to be married

patriot   a person who loves their country

uprising   a revolt against those in power

WILHELM STIEBER, THE PRUSSIAN BLOODHOUND

BACKGROUND

- For 200 years, Germany was a collection of small states.

- In the mid-1800s, the German military leader, Otto von Bismarck, brought these small states together under the leadership of the Prussian king, Wilhelm I.

- Now strong and united, Prussia began invading other countries.

Wilhelm Stieber: 1818–82
Born: Merseburg, Prussia
Spied for Prussia against Austria and France

Lies and schemes

Wilhelm Stieber was a lawyer at a time when poor people in Prussia were trying to force the government to make things better for workers in factories and mines. Stieber represented many poor people in court and saved them from going to prison. Because of this, the workers trusted Stieber and invited him to their secret meetings. Stieber pretended to support the workers. Instead, he betrayed them and passed on their secret plans to the police.

Stieber wins the favor of the king

One day, the Prussian king was out strolling when an angry group of workers threatened him. Stieber appeared, grabbed the king's arm, and pushed him through a doorway, safely out of reach of the mob. The king was so grateful that he rewarded Stieber by making him chief of police. The king did not know that Stieber had organized the whole event.

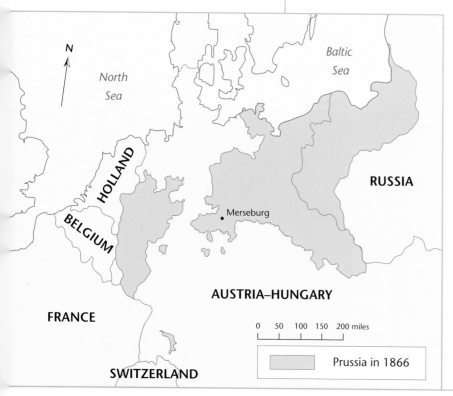

N

North Sea

Baltic Sea

HOLLAND

BELGIUM

FRANCE

• Merseburg

RUSSIA

AUSTRIA–HUNGARY

SWITZERLAND

0   50   100 150   200 miles

Prussia in 1866

Stieber's enemies

Stieber made many enemies as chief of police. In 1858, he fled Prussia in fear of his life. He spent the next five years in Russia running the Russian secret police. The Russians did not like Stieber either, so Stieber set out to make himself useful to Prussia again.

Stieber begins spying on a grand scale

Wilhelm Stieber.

Stieber sent von Bismarck a report on the strength of the whole Russian army. Bismarck liked it. He was planning to invade Austria, and he asked Stieber to put together a similar report on the Austrian army. Stieber filled a suitcase with holy statues and left for Austria. He moved about the countryside pretending to be a religious salesman. All that time, he was really gathering information and recruiting other spies.

One year later, Stieber gave Bismarck the report. Stieber had gathered so much detailed information that Bismarck's invading army defeated Austria in just seven days. Bismarck then sent Stieber into France to do the same thing there. Stieber organized a large spy network. His spies found out many things to help the invading army. To save the Prussian soldiers from having to carry food with them, the spies found out how many cows were in the fields along the roads the army would take, and how much grain the farmers had in their barns. France was defeated as easily as Austria had been.

Stieber spies at home

Stieber came back to Prussia and set up the same large spy network at home. He had a spy in every café, on every street in Prussia. Stieber ended up knowing everyone's secrets, and became more hated than ever. When Stieber died, a large crowd came to his funeral just to make sure he was dead!

Stieber sold holy statues such as this one.

recruiting   gathering helpers or workers

represented   spoke on behalf of another person

SPIES OF THE AMERICAN CIVIL WAR

BACKGROUND

The American Civil War (1861–65) was fought between the Northern and Southern states of America.

It was fought because the North wanted to make changes that the South did not. One of these changes was to end slavery.

Belle Boyd was a Southern spy who later became an actor.

Belle Boyd: 1844–1900
Born: Virginia, U.S.
Spied for the South (the Confederates) against the North (the Unionists)

A daring young woman

Belle Boyd was 17 years old when the American Civil War began. One day, Northern soldiers burst into her home. A soldier knocked down her mother with a rifle butt. Boyd ran for a pistol and shot the man. Because she was so young and pretty, Boyd was not punished for this act.

The Northern soldiers stayed on in her home. Boyd listened to their conversations and learned a lot of important military information. At night, she would sneak away and deliver this information to the Southern army.

One time, Boyd overheard plans to destroy a series of bridges. To get this vital information to the Confederates, she dashed across a field between the two armies in broad daylight. Northern soldiers fired at her, but she reached the Confederate lines safely.

Arrested for spying

Boyd was arrested for spying three times. Each time, the enemy let her go. On her last arrest, a Northern officer fell in love with her and they ran off to England together. After the war, Boyd became an actor. She toured the world speaking about her life as a spy.

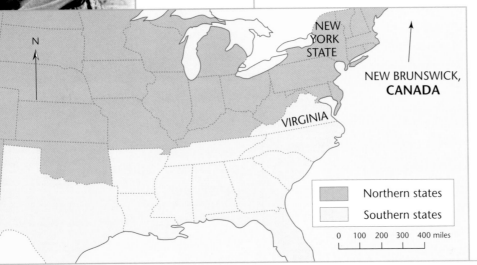

N

NEW YORK STATE

NEW BRUNSWICK, **CANADA**

VIRGINIA

Northern states
Southern states

0   100   200   300   400 miles

Emma Edmonds: 1841–98
Born: New Brunswick, Canada
Spied for the North against the South

Nurse turned spy

Emma Edmonds became a military nurse at the start of the war. At the Battle of Bull Run, she was trapped behind enemy lines but managed to make her way back undetected by Confederate troops. Because she had proved so resourceful, Edmonds was asked to become a spy. On her first mission, she went behind enemy lines disguised as an Afro-American boy. Edmonds spent two years spying and was often disguised as a man. She performed 11 successful missions and was never caught.

Lafayette Baker: 1826–68
Born: New York State, U.S.
Spied for the North against the South

The photographer spy

Lafayette Baker was a photographer who traveled the South taking pictures of soldiers. He listened in on their conversations, and also took note of weapons and troop numbers in the camps. The first time Baker was caught spying, he convinced his Southern captors that he was really spying for them. The second time he was caught, he escaped from prison.

Baker was good at spying and at recruiting other spies. He was put in charge of the whole spy network for the North. His spies, however, failed to uncover the plot against the life of the American president, Abraham Lincoln.

This type of camera was used by Lafayette Baker while spying during the American Civil War.

JAPAN'S BLACK DRAGON SPIES

BACKGROUND

- In the 1890s, Japan began building an empire by first invading Korea and then China.

- Japan wanted Manchuria next.

- Russia also wanted Manchuria, and fought Japan in a war over it from 1904 to 1905.

RUSSIA

MANCHURIA

Sea of Japan

JAPAN

KOREA

Yellow Sea

CHINA

0 100 200 300 400 miles

N

Spying for no payment

The Black Dragon Society was a Japanese spy network set up in 1901. Black Dragon spies were young Japanese men who were willing to spy for their country for no pay. Many Black Dragon spies went to Manchuria disguised as Chinese workers. There they worked on the docks, unloading Russian guns and machinery. This way they found out how many guns the Russians had.

Other Black Dragon spies helped build Russian forts and railroad. Each spy wrote the information he gathered on a tiny piece of rice paper. Teams of three or four runners carried the rice-paper messages back to the Japanese army. Black Dragon spies were so successful that Japan ended up knowing more about the strength of the Russian army and navy than the Russians did.

The Jam Pots spies

A special group of Black Dragon spies went to Manchuria and set up bases called Jam Pots. These were inns where

Russian soldiers came to buy food and drink. The soldiers would sit and gossip while the Japanese storekeepers secretly listened. They learned much valuable information this way.

Two Black Dragon spies being executed by Russian soldiers. Very few Black Dragon spies were caught.

GLOSSARY

ambassador   a person who officially represents a country

armor   metal clothing that protects the body

banish   send away, never to return

broke ranks   broke away from a well-ordered group

code   a secret language

conquistadors   Spanish soldiers who conquered Central America in the 1500s

convincing   making a person believe that what you say is true

disbanded   when a group is broken up

effigy   a model of a person

empire   a large number of countries ruled by one powerful country

evidence   facts that prove the truth

fiancée   a woman engaged to be married

flax   a plant that is dried and woven into rope and mats

forged   faked

gadgets   special tools

into the field   going into other countries to spy

invaded   used force to enter someone else's land

marshes   wet and soggy land

militia   an army of people who are not professional soldiers

minstrel   an old-fashioned singer or musician

Mongol   people from Mongolia

Morse code   signals of dots and dashes that represent letters of the alphabet

patriot   a person who loves their country

peace deal   an agreement not to fight

plague   a deadly disease that spreads from person to person

poverty   poor living conditions

prophets   people who tell the future

recruiting   gathering helpers or workers

represented   spoke on behalf of another person

second in line   the next person to inherit the throne

spooking   frightening

spy master   a person in charge of many spies

translator   a person who changes one language into another

Tsar   a Russian king

uprising   a revolt against those in power

INDEX